THE PRACTICAL JOKER'S HANDBOOK

John Dinneen lives in Cambridge with his wife and son. He started playing practical jokes at a very early age and drove his parents mad in the process. Forced to leave home in his late teens he continued playing jokes on his friends. On occasion they get their own back on him!

Lucy Maddison is a world-famous illustrator and secret practical joker. She lives in London with Pup the cat.

THE
PRACTICAL JOKER'S
HANDBOOK

JOHN DINNEEN

Illustrated by
LUCY MADDISON

SCHOLASTIC INC.
New York Toronto London Auckland Sydney
Mexico City New Delhi Hong Kong Buenos Aires

ISBN 0-439-40491-6

Text copyright © 1996 by John Dinneen. Illustrations copyright © 1996 by Macmillan Children's Books. All rights reserved. Published by Scholastic Inc., 557 Broadway, New York, NY 10012, by arrangement with Macmillan Children's Books. SCHOLASTIC and associated logos are trademarks and/or registered trademarks of Scholastic Inc.

12 11 10 9 8 7   2 3 4 5 6 7/0

Printed in the U.S.A.   40
First Scholastic printing, March 2002

Contents

Rules For Practical Jokers	1
Warning – Keep This Book Dry	3
Train Trip	4
Kilmarnock	5
Join the Club	6
Secret Shakes	7
The Milkshake	8
The Train Shake	9
The Shocker	9
Sausage Finger	10
Dead Hand	11
Sooty	11
Funny Face	12
High Lift	13
Grabber	14
Bag Catch	15
Eggsperts	16
Gniklat Sdrawkcab	17
Cry Baby	18

Wolf Whistle	19
Parrot Shriek	20
Owl Hooter	21
Severed Thumb	22
Balloon Surprise	23
Incredible Feat	24
Tricky Tapper	25
A Sure Bet	26
Dummy	27
Head Tapper	28
Mock Fight	29
The Gentle Ghost	30
Hi Sam!	32
Spooky Face	34
Paper Rain	35
Cracked Glass	36
Smudger	36
Missing Teeth	37
Cracking Egg	38
Broken Nose	39

A Watery Trick   40

Cheeky Echo   41

A Whirligig   42

Black Eye Telescope   44

Apple Pie Bed   45

The Horrid Finger   46

Thumb Stick   48

Tearaway   48

Shrunken Head   49

A Fishy Bite   50

Round The Stick   51

Corker   52

Knock Down   53

Rising Moon   54

Balloons and Buns   56

Sausages   57

One Dark Night   58

Smash It!   60

Silly Shopping   62

Sometimes Practical Joking pays off...   63

Wackier Still   64

I BEG YOUR
FORGIVENESS
YOUR MAJEST

Rules for Practical Jokers

You will have a lot of fun with the practical jokes in this book. They are all harmless but you will be able to bamboozle and befuddle your friends and family with them. There are, however, a few simple rules that practical jokers should always follow:

Choose your victims with care.

Make sure they are someone that will see the funny side of the joke afterwards.

Never play practical jokes on anyone that you think might become upset by it. Upsetting anybody is not a joke, it is just being nasty.

Never try a practical joke that could hurt anyone.

Do not play practical jokes on grown-ups unless you are certain that they will find them funny.

Remember that your victims may well play jokes back on you and then you will have to see the funny side of things!

Lastly, it is a good idea to wear running shoes so you can make a quick getaway!

WARNING –
KEEP THIS BOOK DRY!

This book is environmentally friendly and is printed on especially biodegradable paper made from the Mayog Rocket plant grown in sustainable rain forests of Eastern Peru. Should the pages become damp they will immediately start sprouting shoots and leaves. If this occurs, quickly carry the book/plant outdoors and summon assistance without delay. The publishers can accept no responsibility for damage caused to ceilings or walls, etc. if this rapid growth of vegetation occurs.

SO, YOU HAVE BEEN WARNED – KEEP IT DRY!

Train Trip

Ask a group of people: "Who's good at arithmetic?" Now tell them to listen carefully while you ask them the answer to this problem:

"A train left Edinburgh (*you can make up your own stations*) with ten people on board. At Livingston four passengers got on and three got off." Pause long enough for your audience to work this out then go on to tell how many passengers got on and off at the next five or six stations.

Just when your audience think they have worked out the answer, ask them: "How many times did the train stop?"

Kilmarnock

Here is a very old trick:

Say to a friend: "Kilmarnock is a very long word, spell it."

Every time they write and spell Kilmarnock you say, "No, wrong!" (whether they spell it right or wrong).

When they give up, say all they had to spell was I-T ... IT!

Another tease is to wait for them to spell the letters: K-I-L-M-A-R ... and then shout "No, no, no ...!" They will probably start to spell the word again, and you do exactly the same thing again.

After a few tries they will give up and ask what they are doing wrong. You answer: "Nothing, I was just trying to tell you that the next two letters were N-O, NO!"

Join the Club

In order to join your secret club tell a friend that they have to kiss the mystic book three times while they are blindfolded. If they agree to join then hold out a book while they put the blindfold on. Let them kiss it twice before you swap the book for a plate of flour that you just happened to have hidden nearby!

Secret Shakes

Members of secret societies have special handshakes such as keeping one finger bent or pressing a finger into the other person's palm. Some are said to perform very weird handshakes indeed and can include things like pulling a funny face and saying special greetings.

You and your friends can use secret handshakes and have a go at inventing the weirdest handshakes in the world.

Wacky Handshakes

Here are some weirdly way-out handshakes to surprise your friends.

The Milkshake

Take your friend by the hand and say:

"Good morning (*or afternoon or whatever*), I'm from your local dairy."

Squeeze their hand, then relax, then squeeze again and so on as if you are milking a cow.

The Train Shake

This time take their hand and say:

"Good morning, I'm your friendly railway inspector."

Move their hand and arm vigorously backwards and forwards like a railway engine piston. You can make steam train noises for extra effect

CHUFF CHUFF CHUFF CHUFF

The Shocker

Take your victim by the hand and say:

"Good morning, I'm from the local electricity company."

Press your middle finger into their palm and shake their hand rapidly up and down. At the same time make a loud buzzing noise as if you are giving them a violent electric shock.

Sausage Finger

For this horrid little handshake you will need a raw sausage.

Put the sausage between two of your fingers
so that it looks as though you have
got five fingers and a thumb on
one hand. Now choose a victim
and without them seeing the
sausage shake their hand
and say:

"Ouch! Mind my bad finger."

They will get a nasty shock when you pull your hand away
and leave them holding the sausage!

Dead Hand

Ask a friend: "What's one of these?" (*Hold your hand out with fingers and palm pointing upwards*).

When they give up, say: "A dead one of these!" (*Hold your hand out with fingers and palm pointing downwards.*)

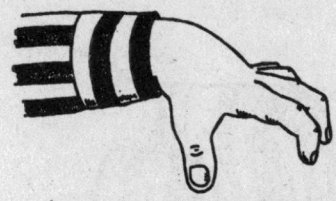

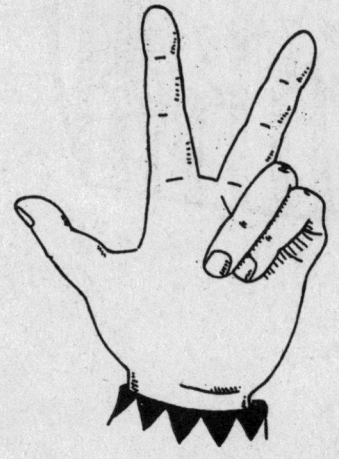

Sooty

Ask a friend: "What's one of these?" (*Hold your hand with your thumb and first two fingers pointing upwards.*)

When they give up, say: "Sooty with no clothes on!"

Funny Face

Paint or stick eyes on your chin, hang upside down and become a silly face. For extra realism you can paint on hair and cover the rest of your face with a handkerchief.

High Lift

Bet a friend that you can lift them high into the air.

First press down on their head with both your hands for ten seconds.

Now tell your friend to close their eyes while you put your hands under their arms and pretend to lift them upwards.

Your victim will feel as if they are being lifted high in the air.

Grabber

Pretend that someone or something hidden behind a door has grabbed you round the neck. (Really you have grabbed yourself round the neck.)

Roll the sleeve up on your grabbing arm so that it looks different to your other arm. You can have quite a tussle with your "assailant".

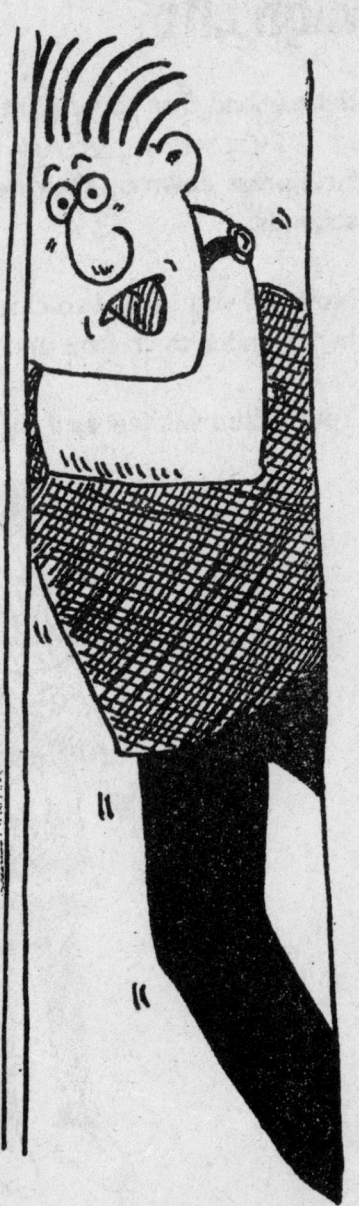

Bag Catch

Hold a paper bag open with your second finger inside it. With your other hand pretend to throw an object up into the air, follow "it" with your eyes, then pretend to catch "it" in the paper bag.

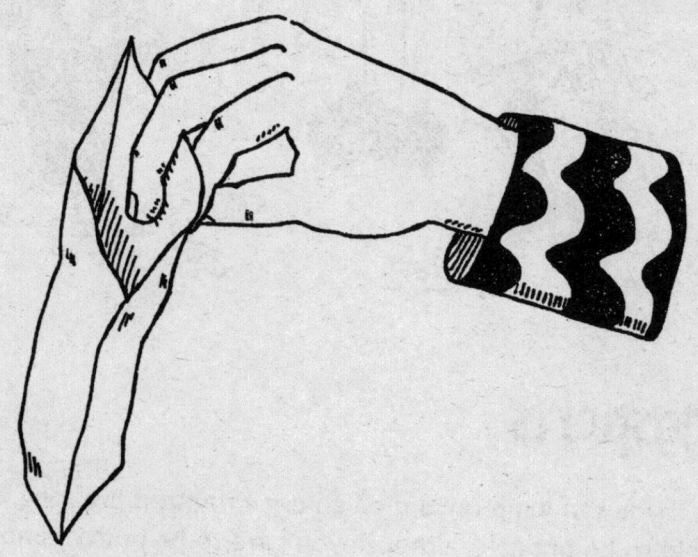

At this point secretly flick the bag with your index finger. This can seem very realistic and after a few "catches" you'll surprise your friends by showing them an empty bag. (You can blow it up and burst it.)

Eggsperts

See if you can jump on and off an egg without it breaking. It is said to be possible, although you have to be pretty nimble. Jump way into the air, over the egg. Before you land on the egg quickly raise your feet into the air and to the sides. With practice your feet should just touch the egg.

You and a friend can also try playing catch with an egg. See how far apart you can stand without the egg breaking.

Both these egg stunts should be performed outdoors.

Gniklat Sdrawkcab

Try saying words backwards and you'll be surprised how quickly you get the hang of it.

You'll find backspeak very useful for talking to friends without others understanding and for being rude to people without them knowing.

Cry Baby

Take your shoes off and put them on a table with your hands inside them.

Then get a friend to put a cardigan round you back to front then stand behind you with their arms in the sleeves.

Now if you start crying, shouting and stamping your "feet" you can give a good imitation of a silly cry baby.

Wolf Whistle

Here's the secret of making a really ear-piercing whistle!

Fold the tip of your tongue back with the tips of the first two fingers of each hand. Keep your finger tips together and pressed onto the underside of your tongue. Now purse your lips and blow along your fingers as hard as you can. With practice and adjustment of your fingers and tongue you will be able to make a high-pitched wolf whistle! You can also use the first and third fingers (hold the second finger out of the way with your thumb) or the thumb and first finger of one hand.

Parrot Shriek

SQUARK!

**This is useful little trick to know if you
ever find yourself lost in the Amazon jungle.**

Open your mouth wide and gently suck
in some air and make a vibrating, growling
noise in your throat. Now if you do the same
thing but this time suck the air very rapidly you
can make a realistic parrot shriek!

Owl Hooter

Here's how to hoot like an owl.

Put your palms and thumbs together and clasp your fingers
round the backs of your hands. Bend your thumbs and make
a hollow between your palms. With your lips round the
knuckles of your thumbs blow between them and make an
eerie owl hoot.

Severed Thumb

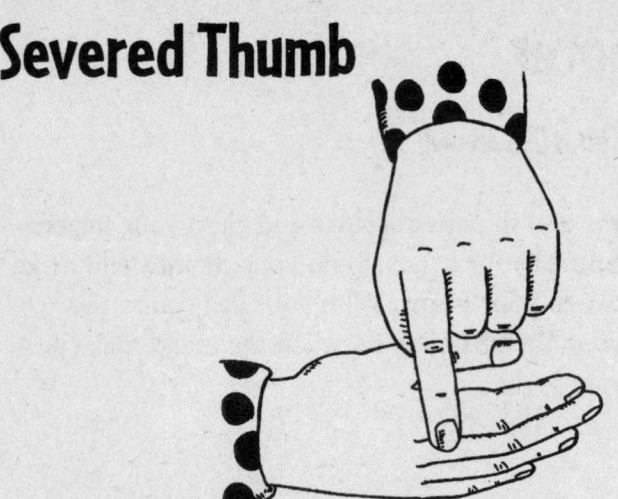

Bend your thumbs in the middle as far as possible then put them together so that they look like one thumb. Hide the join with your first finger then call out: "Help, I've cut my thumb off!" and move your thumbs apart. It can be even more realistic with a "blood-stained" handkerchief wrapped round it.

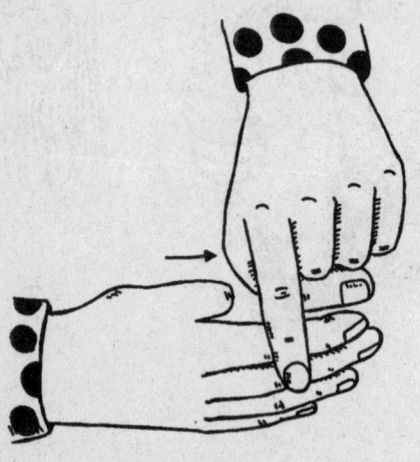

Balloon Surprise

Blow up a balloon and hold it tight to keep the air in. Now slightly open a door and on the outside put the balloon end between the door and the frame.

Carefully shut the door and the balloon should stay there blown up.

Hide, and when an unsuspecting person opens the door the balloon will whiz off – giving them a fright!

Incredible Feat

Tell your friends that you will perform an incredible feat.
Line up three chairs together, eyeing them carefully to make
sure that they are exactly right. Now while still eyeing the
chairs say: "I'll just take my shoes off before I jump over
them" – which you proceed to do exactly. That is, take your
shoes off and jump over them!

Tricky Tapper

Hold a pencil in your left hand, tap it three times on the table and bet someone that they can't do the same. Nine times out of ten your victim will take the pencil in their right hand and then tap it.

If they do, tell them: "No! That's wrong, try again ... and again ... and again!"

A Sure Bet

Bet a friend that they can't answer four questions wrongly. First ask them three easy ones such as: "How old are you? What's your name? Where do you live?"

If they give three wrong answers then pause, look a bit puzzled and say: "That's three questions I've asked, isn't it?"

Your friend should immediately say "Yes" and so answer the fourth question correctly and lose the bet!

Dummy

Sneak up before bedtime and make a dummy in someone's bed.

Stuff their pyjamas with some clothes, use a stuffed T-shirt and mask for a head, etc.

This can give someone quite a shock, especially if the lights are on low.

Head Tapper

It's hard not to laugh when you play this rotten trick.

Get two friends to kneel or sit facing each other each with a plastic spoon in their mouth. Now tell them to take turns to lower their head while their opponent taps them on the head with their spoon to see who can tap the hardest.

In fact it is only possible to give a very gentle tap with a spoon in your mouth. However you can play a trick on one of your friends if you hide a plastic spoon in your hand and your other friend is in on the trick. This time when your victim bends forward, secretly give them a smart tap on the head with your spoon while the other player pretends that they have done it in the usual way. Your victim will be surprised at how hard their adversary managed to tap them and if you continue will bust a gut trying to do the same!

Mock Fight

Shock everyone by fighting a friend!

Pretend to argue with a friend, then give them a pretend slap which leads to a fight with more "slaps" or "punches".

Every time someone is hit make a slapping noise by secretly clapping your hands together. Make it as painful as possible – yell things like: "Ow! That hurts! I'll get you for that!" … etc, etc.

A mock fight can look very realistic – in fact just like the ones staged on film and television.

The Gentle Ghost

Give someone a fright with this creepy trick.

Choose a victim and sit opposite them.

Explain that there is a gentle ghost in the room that sometimes appears if the conditions are right.

Put a hand over each of your victim's eyes and then an index finger on each closed eyelid. After a short while remove your hands and explain that the ghost is more likely to appear if they relax.

Put your fingers on their eyelids again, making sure that they first see that you are using both your hands. After a short while remove your hands again.

Now tell them that you can feel the ghost is quite close. This time when your victim closes their eyes place a finger and thumb of one hand on their eyelids.

Wait a while then quietly move your spare hand to the back of your victim's head and touch their hair or neck very gently – giving them a hair-raising fright!

Hi Sam!

Get ready to run after trying out this cheeky stunt.

Clap a friend on the shoulder and say and do the following things quickly:

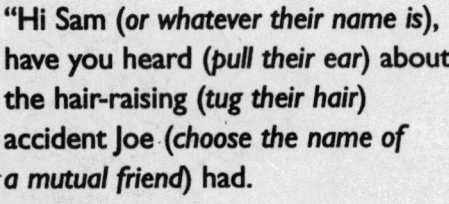

"Hi Sam (*or whatever their name is*), have you heard (*pull their ear*) about the hair-raising (*tug their hair*) accident Joe (*choose the name of a mutual friend*) had.

"He/she put his/her jumper on back (*clap them on the back*) to front (*clap them on the chest*) and couldn't see (*put your hand over their eyes*) a thing.

"He/she fell (*keeping your hand over their eyes, push them forward with your other hand on the back of their head*) into a pond and got completely soaked from head (*tap them on the head*) to toe (*tread on their toes*).

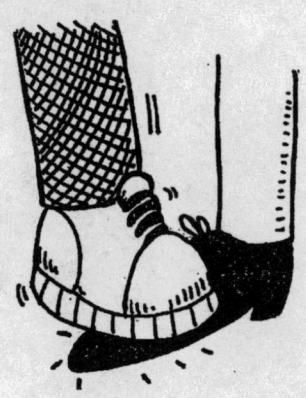

"Anyway cheerio Sam, I must rush off now." (*Give them a last slap on the shoulder and run off as fast as you can!*)

Spooky Face

Give someone a night-time fright!

Hold a torch just below your chin so that the light shines up at your face. This can look very spooky especially if you pull a horrible face at the same time.

Paper Rain

Put some confetti inside someone's umbrella and then roll it up again. When your victim opens their umbrella they will think they are in a paper storm. (You can make your own confetti by tearing paper into very small pieces.)

Cracked Glass

Chisel a point on a bar of soap then use it to draw a "crack" on a mirror or window pane. It can look very realistic so get ready for some fireworks!

Smudger

Pretend to remove a smudge from someone's face while secretly adding some of your own. You can use things like soot, mascara, lipstick, etc.

Missing Teeth

Make photographs more interesting by sticking small pieces of black paper on some of your front teeth. When you grin it will look as though these teeth are missing.

Cracking Egg

Pretend to crack an egg over someone's head and see if they get the yoke.

Tell your victim that you are going to crack an egg over their head. (You can show them a real egg to make it even more realistic.)

Go behind your victim, put the finger tips of one of your hands together and lightly place them on the top of their head, pretending you are holding an egg.

Smartly tap the back of this hand with your other one and slowly open out your fingers in your victim's hair as the "egg" breaks.

Now gently, using both hands, move your fingers down their hair and neck, pretending it is the runny egg. This can feel very realistic.

Broken Nose

Horrify someone with this trick.

Tell an adult or a friend that you think you have broken your nose.

Put your hands either side of your nose with your fingers pointing upwards.

You will now be able to make a clicking noise by secretly clicking one of your thumbnails against your top teeth.

Keeping your hands together waggle your nose with them while at the same time making the loud clicking noise as if your nose is cracking!

A Watery Trick

Give a friend this tricky problem to solve.

Fill two paper cups with water.

Put them on the backs of your friend's hands.

Now tell him or her to remove both cups without spilling any water.

The answer is to carefully drink the water in one cup and then remove the other with the free hand. It is best to try this out in the kitchen!

Cheeky Echo

Choose an echo-y sort of place, such as a corridor, hall or archway, etc. and get a friend to hide at one end.

Now choose a victim, explain that there is a tremendous echo in here and get them to stand at the other end of the corridor. Your hidden friend must echo the end of anything your victim shouts out, for example:

"Hello there!" – "… o there!"
"How are you?" – "… are you?" … and so on.

Of course, after a few realistic echoes the echo can produce a cheeky answer.

A Whirligig

Give your friends a fright with this devilish device!

You will need: two pieces of paper and a small elastic band.

How to make a Whirligig

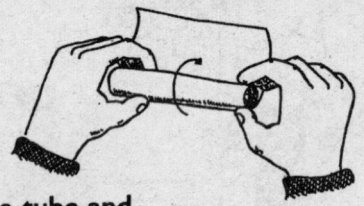

Roll each piece of paper into a tube and
then twist each tube in the middle.

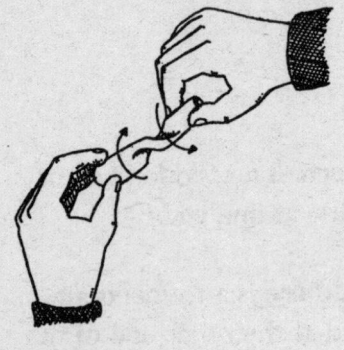

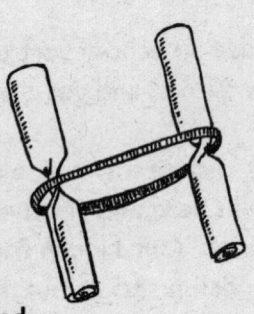

Put the twists through the elastic band.
Next, hold one twist firmly and wind the other
one round until it's tight.

Now carefully place your wound-up whirligig
under a heavy object such as a book.
Watch the fun when somebody lifts the book!

Black Eye Telescope

You will need a cardboard tube (for example from a kitchen roll) and some poster paint.

Paint the tube with black poster paint and allow it to dry. When you are ready to play the trick on someone paint the end of the tube with more poster paint.

Tell your victim that you have a magic telescope. When they look down the painted end the result will be a black eye.

Apple Pie Bed

Fold the bottom sheet in half so that both ends are at the pillow end of the bed, and tuck the sides in as usual.

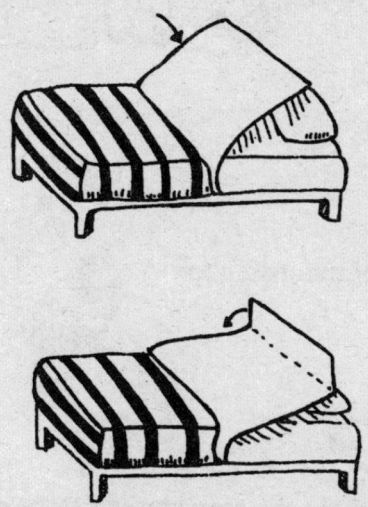

When the top covers are replaced, the single sheet will now look like a top and bottom sheet and it will be impossible for anybody to get in!

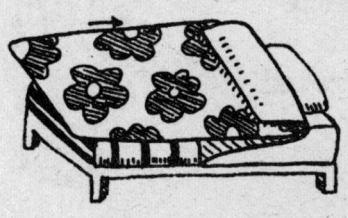

The Horrid Finger

You will need:
A matchbox
Red ink
Cotton wool
Talcum powder

Remove one end of the matchbox
tray with scissors.

Line the matchbox bottom with cotton
wool splattered with a little red ink.

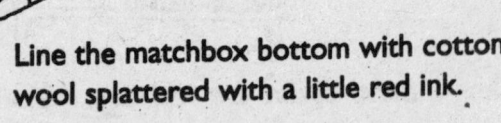

For a grim effect, dust your
index finger with white
talcum powder and
splatter a little more red
ink around its base.

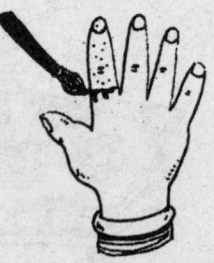

Shut the matchbox and put your finger in the open end.
Tell your victim that you have found
someone's finger on the floor ...
Slide open the matchbox and
reveal the finger inside.

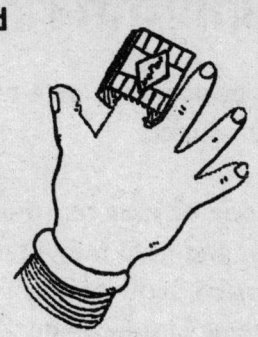

Thumb Stick

Use a peeler to carve a potato into the same size and shape as your thumb.

Bend one of your real thumbs out of sight and hold the potato one in its place. Now horrify your friends by sticking pins into your "thumb".

You can cover your potato thumb with a handkerchief before sticking pins into it and secretly remove it when you lift off the handkerchief.

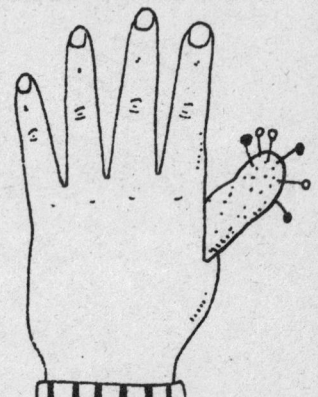

Tearaway

If someone is showing off their money, grab hold of a note, hold it up to your mouth and quickly pretend to tear it in half. At the same time blow hard at the edge of the note to make a realistic tearing sound!

Shrunken Head

You will need: a large apple or potato, some hair clippings and glue.

Carefully carve the apple into a head shape with sunken eyes. Now leave it for at least several days to dry out. When it is dry and brown stick the hair clippings on top – you are now the proud owner of a shrunken head!

Wrap it in a handkerchief and present it to your mum saying, "Look what I swapped with Amy" (or whoever). As she unwraps it, quickly shout out: "It's a shrunken head!"

A Fishy Bite

Here is a trick to try if there is a tank of goldfish around.

Carefully cut a carrot into thin fish-shaped slices.
(You can get an adult to help you do this.)

Now wrap your fishy slices in a handkerchief and
carry them along to the fish tank. Hide one of the
slices in your hand and when someone comes along
plunge part of your hand in the water and pretend to pull
out a "wriggling goldfish" (which is in fact of course your
shaking carrot slice). Triumphantly hold the still "wriggling
goldfish" in the air before popping it in your
mouth and chewing it up.

This should produce shock and horror in
the onlooker which is only made worse
when you say: "Yum, that was lovely. I think
I'll have another" ... and repeat
the process.

Party Joker

Here are some games with a catch that will liven up any party.

Round the Stick

Challenge your friends to this spinning trick.

You will need: a walking stick or umbrella.

Hold the walking stick upright on the floor. Get your first victim to place the palm of their right hand on top of it, the left hand on top of their right and then bend over and put their forehead on top of their hands.

Now tell them to close their eyes and walk briskly round the stick three times while the stick remains upright.

When they have done this, immediately tell them to walk to an object, such as a chair on the other side of the room — and watch the fun!

Corker

This zany game will leave everyone tongue-tied.

You will need: a cork and a piece of
tissue paper for each person.

Fold a piece of tissue paper round one end of each cork and
give one to each player. Explain that they must hold the end
with the tissue paper in their mouths, but must not touch
the tissue paper with their tongues. Anyone
with wet tissue paper at the end
of the game will be disqualified.

Everyone will have a hoot trying to
talk to one another. When you feel
that they have "mastered" cork-talking
you can hold a competition. Players
take turns to sing a song or say a few sentences —
the winner is the person that everyone understands
the best.

Knock Down

Here's how to knock all your friends over at the same time.

Bet your friends that they can't copy everything you can do.

Get them to line up shoulder to shoulder facing the same way, with you at one end.

Now say, "I'm kneeling down on my right knee" and do it. Check that everyone else is doing the same.

Now say, "I'm raising my right arm" and do it and check the others again.

Keeping your right arm raised, say, "I'm now raising my left arm" and do it.

Turn as if to check that the others are doing the same but quickly give the person nearest to you a firm push. With luck the whole row of your friends will topple over and end up sprawled over the floor!

Rising Moon

You will need:
A torch
A sheet
A cold, wet sponge or flannel
Three assistants

Turn the lights down low and ask two of your assistants to hold the sheet between them so that it is at chest height.

The third assistant goes behind the sheet with the torch and with the wet sponge hidden nearby. Then they shine the torch through the sheet near the floor.

Tell the first player to put their nose on the moon and follow it as the assistant moves the torch to the top of the sheet with a slow zig-zag movement.

Players take turns to see who can follow the moon the closest.

As the last player's nose reaches the top of the sheet the assistant sploshes the wet sponge into their face!

Balloons and Buns

This sticky game will have everyone in fits.

You will need: a balloon and a sticky bun for each player. (For a less messy version use two cream crackers in place of each bun.)

Everyone sits down with a balloon and a bun. Explain that when you call "Bite" they have to take a big bite of bun and chew it as quickly as they can, and that when you call "Blow" they have to start blowing up their balloon.

Tell them that anyone getting it wrong will be disqualified and the winner will be the person who finishes the bun first and has the biggest balloon.

Start off slowly: "Bite ... blow ... bite ..." Then you can get a bit faster and mix it up a bit: "Bite, blow, blow, bite, bite ..."

Soon you'll have them trying to blow up their buns and bite their balloons!

Sausages

This joke could turn someone as red as a beetroot.

Pretend to whisper something to each of your friends in turn. When you come to your victim whisper in his or her ear: "Everybody's going to yell out SAUSAGES! when I raise my hand."

Now wait for a suitably embarrassing moment, then lift up your hand and look as if you are about to shout out and with luck your victim will yell out "SAUSAGES!" – all on their own.

One Dark Night

Put the wind up everyone with this spooky tale.

You will need: an assistant with a sheet who secretly waits outside the room.

(It is a good idea to first practise reading the story slowly and make sure your assistant knows what he or she has to do.)

Get everyone to sit round in a semi-circle. Explain that you are going to tell them a spooky story and that you will raise your hand every time a noise is mentioned. Everyone must imitate the noise until you put your hand down.

It will be even more spooky if the lights are turned down low. Now begin telling the story, making it as scary as you can:

One dark night I was woken by the wind WHISTLING down the chimney and RATTLING the window panes. An owl HOOTED. A dog HOWLED. Suddenly there was a loud CLAP of thunder followed by a noise like FIENDISH LAUGHING. I sat up in bed, trembling.

Somewhere a door BANGED. Then another door BANGED. Somebody or something was downstairs! Then the stairs CREAKED ... the CREAKING got louder: the thing was coming up the stairs!

To pretend I wasn't frightened I tried to HUM A TUNE,
then another different TUNE, but when I stopped there
were heavy FOOTSTEPS in the hall. I hid under the bed
covers but still heard those sounds that I will never forget:
a HORRIBLE GROWL followed by a TERRIFYING SCREAM!

Suddenly the door handle CREAKED VIOLENTLY as it
turned! There was a loud thud on the door (*your assistant
bangs on the door outside and you can pretend to look scared at
this point*). Then more thuds (*again your assistant bangs*).
Suddenly the door burst open! (*Now your assistant, wearing a
white sheet, bursts into the room — scaring everyone to death!*)

Smash It!

It's surprising how upset people get when you "smash their watch to smithereens".

You will need: a handkerchief. (A mallet is optional.)

Sit at a table and tell everyone that you can show them a brilliant trick if somebody lends you their watch. Stress that they will have their watch back safe and sound afterwards.

Lay out the handkerchief near the edge of the table, put the watch in the middle and fold the top edge over the bottom.

Then fold the two sides over.

Now lift the handkerchief a little bit and secretly let the watch slide out of the end onto your lap. Then fold the bottom edge of the handkerchief over the top.

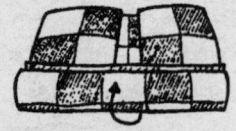

Everyone will now think that the watch is safely wrapped up in the handkerchief. Tell them you are going to smash the watch and then magic it whole again.

Hit the handkerchief hard several times with your fist or mallet. Then hit it a few times more just to make sure. Reassure your victim that there is nothing to worry about as the trick works every time.

Slowly begin to unwrap the handkerchief. Suddenly look worried and pretend that the trick has gone wrong.

Hastily wrap up the handkerchief, saying things like: "I can't understand what's happened this time ... I've got a spare watch at home that you could have ...,"

Your victim will be quite upset at this stage, but can be put out of their misery by showing them their watch magically whole again! To do this secretly, take the watch in your hand, unfold the handkerchief over this hand, then reveal the watch.

Silly Shopping

Ask an innocent victim to buy something for you from a shop. The catch is that the "thing" doesn't exist. Here are some suggestions: A sky hook, elbow grease, striped paint, left-handed pencils, cockerel's eggs, pigeon's milk, etc.

Or you can make up a silly title for a book or tape and then ask a victim to buy it for you.

Sometimes Practical Joking pays off ...

Some years ago a prankster named David Shwartz started a collection of beat-up old bangers. As a joke he advertised them for rent. To his surprise people liked hiring them and the business thrived. It seemed that his customers liked the fact that it didn't matter if they damaged the car a bit and soon our enterprising joker had many Rent-a-Wreck branches all over the USA.

King Henry VIII of England was said to have been a keen practical joker. He would set up a life-size portrait of himself which visitors would be presented to. In the dim light they might easily think they were in front of the King himself and end up begging for his mercy, taking his lack of movement to be displeasure. Even if they saw through the joke it was probably sensible to pretend otherwise rather than risk literally losing their head.

I BEG YOUR
FORGIVENESS
YOUR MAJESTY

Wackier Still

If you thought that some of the stunts in this book were pretty wacky then what about ...

... The students who secretly painted human feet on their absent-minded professor's black shoes then covered them with water-soluble black paint. When he went out in the rain he couldn't understand why everyone was laughing at him ...

... Or the practical jokers who removed the engine from their car, pushed it to a garage, told the mechanics that it had just broken down and could they fix it for them?

... Or what about the luminous sundials for night use that someone designed as a practical joke? The idea was taken up with the media and some bright spark had 150,000 of them made in Hong Kong ... Apparently they sold like hot cakes!

In fact the media often put out some pretty wacky stories. For example on the first of April a newspaper claimed ...

... that the search was on for the iceberg that sank the Titanic!

Another said that the Italian spaghetti harvest had failed. Bad weather had caused the unripened pasta to fall off the trees before it could be harvested!

Even wackier is the League for Animal Decency in the USA that insists all animals should wear clothes. Dogs and cats, they say, should wear trousers and cows ought to have special brassieres made for them!

Sometimes it's tricky know whether something is a practical joke or not ...

For example, what do you think causes the mysterious corn circles that appear in wheat fields every year? Their large geometric patterns are properly visible only from the air ...

Do you think they are the work of human practical jokers? Or are you one of those who believe they must be the work of alien jokers from outer space?

Well, alien or not, we hope you have enjoyed this book and wish you every success in the future with your own practical jokes.